Just Dance

Irish Dance

Wendy Hinote Lanier
and Madeline Nixon

AV2

Step 1
Go to **www.av2books.com**

Step 2
Enter this unique code

NMDTWXB2H

Step 3
Explore your interactive eBook!

AV2 is optimized for use on any device

Your interactive eBook comes with...

Contents
Browse a live contents page to easily navigate through resources

Audio
Listen to sections of the book read aloud

Videos
Watch informative video clips

Weblinks
Gain additional information for research

Try This!
Complete activities and hands-on experiments

Key Words
Study vocabulary, and complete a matching word activity

Quizzes
Test your knowledge

Slideshows
View images and captions

... and much, much more!

Irish Dance

Contents

Chapter 1

What is Irish Dance?

A dancer takes the stage. Then, two more join him. Their arms stay at their sides. But their legs are moving fast. Their feet strike the ground in **unison**. The crowd cannot get enough of the Irish dancers.

Footwork is the focal point of Irish dance.

There are two main types of Irish dancing. Some Irish dances are **social**. Others are for performance. Both began in the 1700s with dance masters. Dance masters were traveling dance teachers. They traveled among Irish villages and taught people how to dance.

The masters developed group dances. These became known as figure dances. People performed them at social gatherings called ceilis (*kay*-leez). Figure dances are performed in **formations**. Some have as few as two dancers. Others have large groups. The steps are simple. That means anyone can learn them.

Dance Tip

Do not worry about learning the steps before joining figure dances. Simply learn as you go.

Irish dance is often done for parades.

There are five types of Irish dance. Step dance is one of the most popular. The others are ceilis, festival, sean-nos, and Irish set dance.

Dance masters also challenged each other to dance contests. Their solo dances are today's step dances. These dances include jigs and reels. **Hornpipes** are step dances, too. These dances require lots of skill. They can be performed solo or in groups. They can be performed in shows for the public. They can also be in a competition.

More than **500,000 PEOPLE** attend the St. Patrick's Day parade in Dublin, Ireland, and watch its Irish dancers.

The Irish Dancing Commission created the Irish Dancing World Championship in **1970**. It draws about **6,000 COMPETITORS** from **30 COUNTRIES** each year.

Irish Dance Timeline

Irish dance has grown immensely from its origins in Ireland. Due to **immigration** and the strength of Irish **culture**, Irish dance is now performed around the world. The dance has evolved from its beginnings with dance masters who travel and teach in Ireland, to dancers currently performing shows and dancing in parades.

1700s

Dance masters travel across Ireland, teaching reels and jigs.

1845

Masses of Irish people immigrate to places around the world due to lack of food in Ireland. They bring Irish dance with them.

1893

The Gaelic League is formed to promote the Irish identity. It creates its own ceilis and encourages dance competitions and lessons.

People of any age can start learning Irish dance.

1930s

Rules for competition, such as scoring, are established.

1990s

Shows such as *Riverdance* and Michael Flatley's *Lord of the Dance* popularize Irish dance.

Today

Irish dance is more popular than ever. Besides in competitions, Irish dance can be seen at festivals, weddings, holiday shows, and parades.

Irish dancers dress in
easy-to-move clothes.

Chapter 2

Dress Like You Are Irish

In group dances, costumes are based on **traditional** Irish dress. Women might wear simple dresses or skirts. The dresses feature **embroidered Celtic** designs. A **brooch** is pinned at the shoulder. It secures a cape.

Men wear **kilts** or pants. They also wear jackets. The jacket has a folded cloak draped from the shoulder.

Step dancers wear soft shoes for reels and jigs. For other dances, hard shoes are better. Hard shoes have toe tips. Their heels are hollow. The design accents the sounds of the footwork in hornpipes. For figure dances, it is best to wear leather-soled shoes. They let dancers glide on the floor.

Soft shoes are easier to move in for reels and jigs.

Dance Tip

Wear layers when performing in an Irish ceili. You can peel off the layers as you heat up.

Chapter 3

Steps and Figures

I rish step dances are performed on the balls of the feet. These dances require good **stamina**. You must be able to kick high. Your footwork must be precise. You need to move at a fast pace. Posture is important, too. Your upper body should be upright. You must also keep your arms by your sides.

Irish dance takes a lot of hard work.

Figure dances are the traditional dances of Ireland. They are more relaxed. Their steps are usually easier than those in step dancing.

Figure dances have names such as the Bonfire and Haymakers' Jig. Fairy Reel and the Siege of Ennis are figure dances, too.

Dance Tip

In step dancing, arms are carried close to the sides with fists closed. Try holding a coin in each hand to remind yourself to keep your fists closed.

Irish dance can be done alone or in groups.

Irish dancing is a fun way
to spend time with friends.

Another type of dancing is called *sean-nós* (*shan*-nohs). It is a traditional style of solo dancing. The step is relaxed and low to the ground. This makes it similar to tap dancing. Dancers make up the moves as they keep time to the music. The footwork is called battering.

Sean-nós dancers originally danced on wooden doors or barrel tops. This is why today's sean-nós dances are still performed in small spaces.

Irish Jig

An Irish jig starts with the left foot pointed forward.

1. Step forward onto the left foot. Bring your right foot in behind it.

2. Shift your weight to your right foot. Now bring your left toe up to your right knee as you hop.

3. While hopping, kick your left foot out in front of you.

4. Take four steps back, starting with your left foot. The fourth step ends on your right foot. This lets you point your left foot forward and start again.

Riverdance still tours today.

Chapter 4

On with the Show!

In 1994, there was a popular song contest in Dublin, Ireland. A group of Irish dancers performed during **intermission**. Riverdance took off from there. A full-length show began in Dublin the next year. It helped make Irish dancing popular around the world.

Riverdance features upbeat music and dance. Dancers perform their steps in unison. It is hard to take your eyes off them. But Irish dancing does not have to be so formal. And you do not need to be Irish, either. Anyone can join the fun of an Irish social dance. It is as simple as finding a local ceili. Most Irish towns host ceilis in the summer. They welcome visitors. But ceilis can also be found outside Ireland. An Internet search will help you find them.

Dance Tip

To keep a good posture, pull your shoulders back and down. Do not forget to relax.

Irish dancing is common at
Saint Patrick's Day celebrations.

Irish dancers also compete. Competitions usually feature step dancing. To learn step dancing, you can contact your local dance studio. Most dancing schools today offer some type of Irish dance lessons.

The Riverdance show has visited **450** theaters worldwide and been viewed by **25 MILLION** people.

WORLD RECORD

On July of 2013, **1,693** people gathered to set the world record for the longest Riverdance ever.

Irish dancers take part in the World Irish Dancing Championships yearly.

Quiz

1 How many kinds of shoes are worn in Irish step dancing?

2 How many people set the record for longest Riverdance chain?

3 Why are sean-nós performed in small spaces?

4 What are ceilis?

5 Where do your arms typically go during Irish dance?

6 What do men wear to Irish dance?

7 At which parade is Irish dance regularly performed?

8 What are hornpipes?

9 What is typically embroidered on an Irish dance dress?

10 What did dance masters do?

ANSWERS

1. Three **2.** 1,693 **3.** They were originally danced on doors. **4.** Social gatherings with Irish dance **5.** At your sides **6.** Kilts or pants and jackets **7.** St. Patrick's Day parade **8.** Step dances **9.** Celtic designs **10.** Travel and teach dance

Key Words

brooch a piece of jewelry pinned to clothing and worn as a decoration

Celtic having to do with the cultures of Ireland, Scotland, and Wales

culture beliefs, customs, art, and social interactions of a certain group of people

embroidered having designs sewn onto a piece of cloth

formations arrangements of people in groups

hornpipes lively dances that were a favorite of sailors

immigration when a person moves from their home country to another country

intermission a pause in an activity such as between acts of a play

kilts skirts that reach the knees, often worn by Irish or Scottish men

social having to do with activities involving other people

stamina the ability to continue working for a long time

traditional well established within a group of people

unison at the same time

Index

Get the best of both worlds.

AV2 bridges the gap between print and digital.

The expandable resources toolbar enables quick access to content including **videos**, **audio**, **activities**, **weblinks**, **slideshows**, **quizzes**, and **key words**.

Animated videos make static images come alive.

Resource icons on each page help readers to further **explore key concepts**.

Published by AV2
350 5th Avenue, 59th Floor
New York, NY 10118
Website: www.av2books.com

Library of Congress Cataloging-in-Publication Data
Names: Lanier, Wendy Hinote, author.
Title: Irish dance / Wendy Hinote Lanier and Madeline Nixon.
Description: New York, NY : AV2, 2020. | Series: Just dance | Includes
   index. | Audience: Ages 8-12 | Audience: Grades 4-6
Identifiers: LCCN 2020001619 (print) | LCCN 2020001620 (ebook) | ISBN
   9781791123284 (library binding) | ISBN 9781791123291 (paperback) | ISBN
   9781791123307 | ISBN 9781791123314
Subjects: LCSH: Folk dancing, Irish--Juvenile literature. |
   Dance--Ireland--Juvenile literature.
Classification: LCC GV1646.I8 L36 2020 (print) | LCC GV1646.I8 (ebook) |
   DDC 793.3/1415--dc23
LC record available at https://lccn.loc.gov/2020001619
LC ebook record available at https://lccn.loc.gov/2020001620

Printed in Guangzhou, China
1 2 3 4 5 6 7 8 9 0   24 23 22 21 20

022020
101319

Project Coordinator: Heather Kissock   Designer: Ana María Vidal

Every reasonable effort has been made to trace ownership and to obtain permission to reprint copyright material. The publishers would be pleased to have any errors or omissions brought to their attention so that they may be corrected in subsequent printings.

Weigl acknowledges Getty Images, Alamy, Newscom, and Shutterstock as its primary image suppliers for this title.

First published by North Star Editions in 2018.